Zoom In on Polar Animals

Caribou

Leo Statts

abdopublishing.com

Published by Abdo Zoom™, PO Box 398166, Minneapolis, Minnesota 55439. Copyright © 2017 by
Abdo Consulting Group, Inc. International copyrights reserved in all countries. No part of this book may be
reproduced in any form without written permission from the publisher. Abdo Zoom™ is a trademark and logo
of Abdo Consulting Group, Inc.

Printed in the United States of America, North Mankato, Minnesota
062016
092016

Cover Photo: Pim Leijen/Shutterstock Images, cover
Interior Photos: iStockphoto, 1, 7, 8, 16; Paul Wilson/iStockphoto, 5; Karl Umbriaco/Shutterstock Images, 6;
Robert Haasmann/Shutterstock Images, 9; Shutterstock Images, 10–11; Red Line Editorial, 11, 20 (left), 20 (right),
21 (left), 21 (right); Sergey Krasnoshchokov/Shutterstock Images, 12–13; Peter Zelei/iStockphoto, 14; Liz Leyden/
iStockphoto, 15; FloridaStock/Shutterstock Images, 18; ReimPhoto/iStockphoto, 19

Editor: Emily Temple
Series Designer: Madeline Berger
Art Direction: Dorothy Toth

Publisher's Cataloging-in-Publication Data
Names: Statts, Leo, author.
Title: Caribou / by Leo Statts.
Description: Minneapolis, MN : Abdo Zoom, [2017] | Series: Polar animals |
    Includes bibliographical references and index.
Identifiers: LCCN 2016941137 | ISBN 9781680791877 (lib. bdg.) |
    ISBN 9781680793550 (ebook) | ISBN 9781680794441 (Read-to-me ebook)
Subjects: LCSH: Caribou--Juvenile literature. | Reindeer--Juvenile literature.
Classification: DDC 599.65--dc23
LC record available at http://lccn.loc.gov/2016941137

Table of Contents

Caribou

Caribou are deer.
They are also called reindeer.
Both males and females
have **antlers**.

No other female deer have antlers.

Body

Caribou have long fur.

Their **hooves** are wide.
They have two toes.

Caribou grow antlers
around age two.

The antlers fall off each year.
Then they grow back.

Habitat

Caribou live in polar areas.
It is cold there. They live in forests.
They live in **grasslands**.

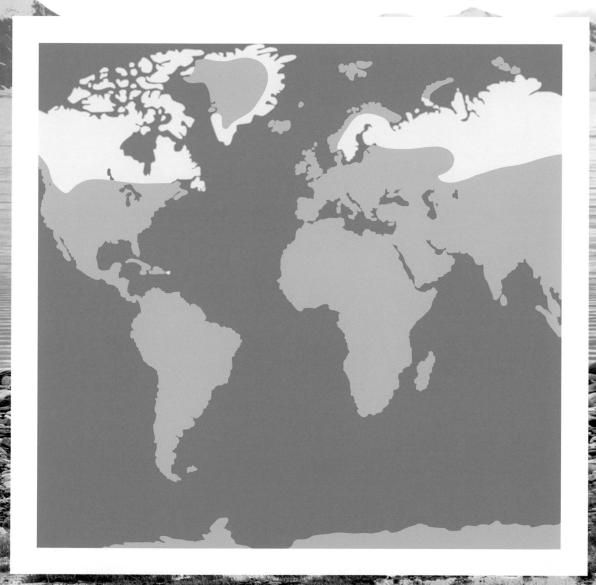

Where caribou live

Caribou live in **herds**.
Herds can have many caribou.

They **migrate** in the winter.
They travel farther than
any other land animal.

Food

Caribou eat plants.
They eat grass and shrubs.

Caribou use their hooves.
They dig through snow.
This helps them find food.

Life Cycle

Baby caribou are **calves**.
They can stand almost right away.

Caribou can live up to 15 years in the wild.

Average Length

A male caribou is almost as long as a sofa.

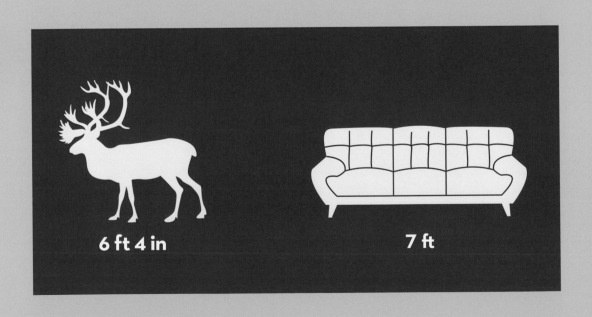

6 ft 4 in

7 ft

Average Weight

A male caribou is heavier than a refrigerator.

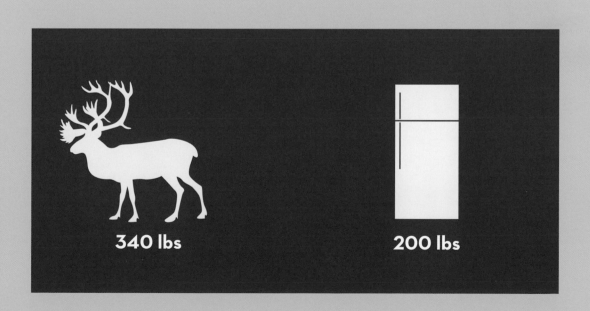

340 lbs   200 lbs

Glossary

antlers – bones that grow from a deer's head.

calf – a baby animal.

grassland - a large area of grass, with little or no trees.

herd - a group of animals.

hooves - hard coverings that protect an animal's feet.

migrate - to move from one place to another, often to find food or water.

Booklinks

For more information
on **caribou**, please visit
booklinks.abdopublishing.com

Zoom™ In on Animals!

Learn even more with the Abdo Zoom
Animals database. Check out
abdozoom.com for more information.

Index